Abbreviations

1 lb .... pound
C .... degrees Celsius
Qt .... quart
c .... cup
in. .... inch
F .... degrees Fahrenheit
tsp or t .... teaspoon
L .... liter
gal .... gallon
tbs .... tablespoon
Fl. oz .... fluid ounce
Pt .... pint
Doz .... dozen (equals 12)

Common Substitutions

Ingredient	Substitution
1 tsp allspice	½ t cinnamon + ½ tsp ground cloves
1 tsp baking powder	½ tsp baking soda + ½ tsp cream of tartar
1 tbs butter	1 T oil, or 1 T shortening
1 cup buttermilk	1 cup milk + 1 tbs vinegar
1 cup heavy cream (not for whipping cream)	¾ cup milk + ⅓ cup butter
1 tsp dried herbs	1 tsp fresh herbs
1 cup self-rising flour	1 cup flour + 1½ tsp baking powder ½ tsp salt
1 tbs lemon juice	½ tbs vinegar
1 cup brown sugar	1 cup sugar or ⅞ cup sugar + 1 tbs molasses

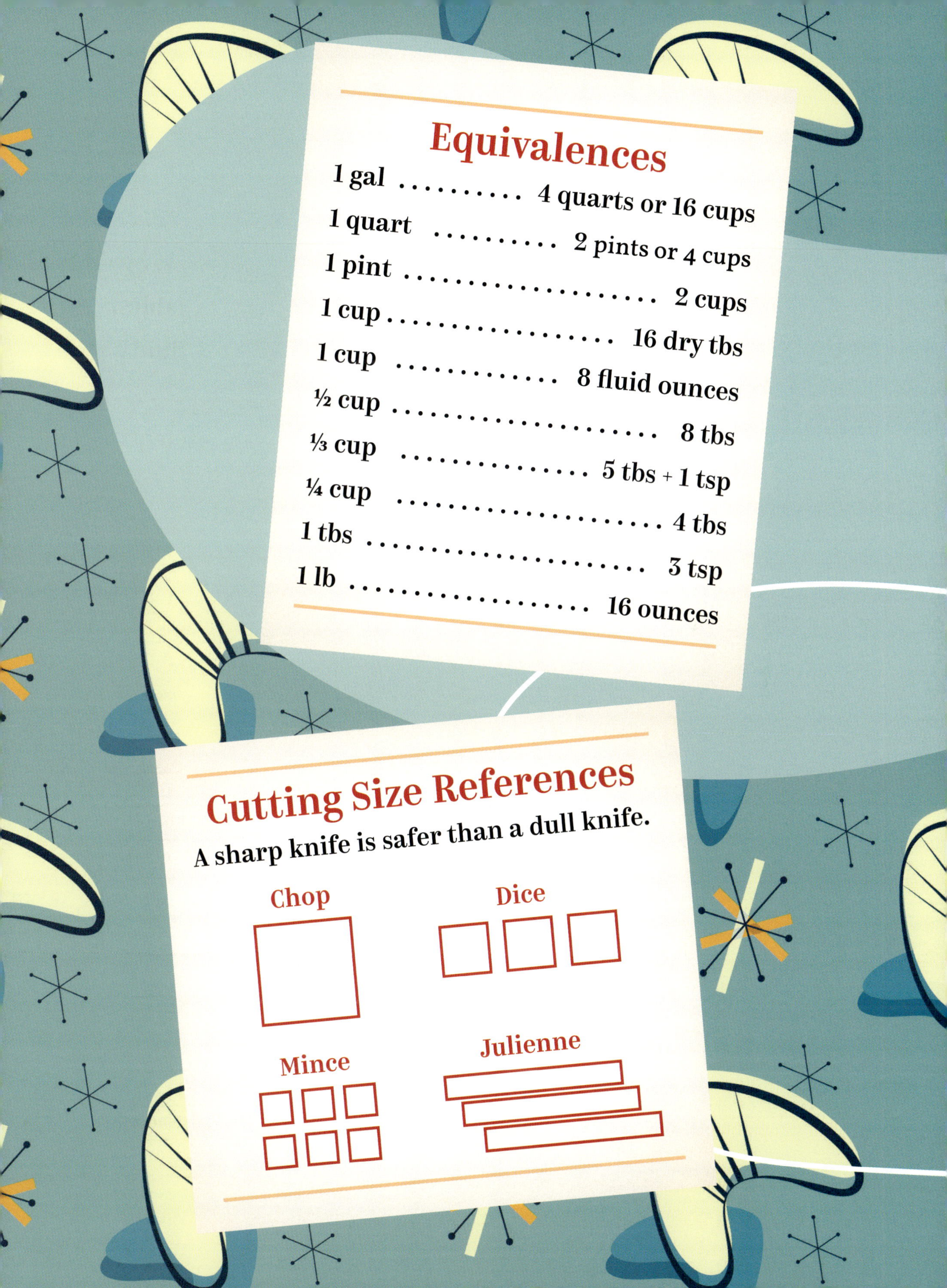

Equivalences

1 gal	4 quarts or 16 cups
1 quart	2 pints or 4 cups
1 pint	2 cups
1 cup	16 dry tbs
1 cup	8 fluid ounces
½ cup	8 tbs
⅓ cup	5 tbs + 1 tsp
¼ cup	4 tbs
1 tbs	3 tsp
1 lb	16 ounces

Cutting Size References

A sharp knife is safer than a dull knife.

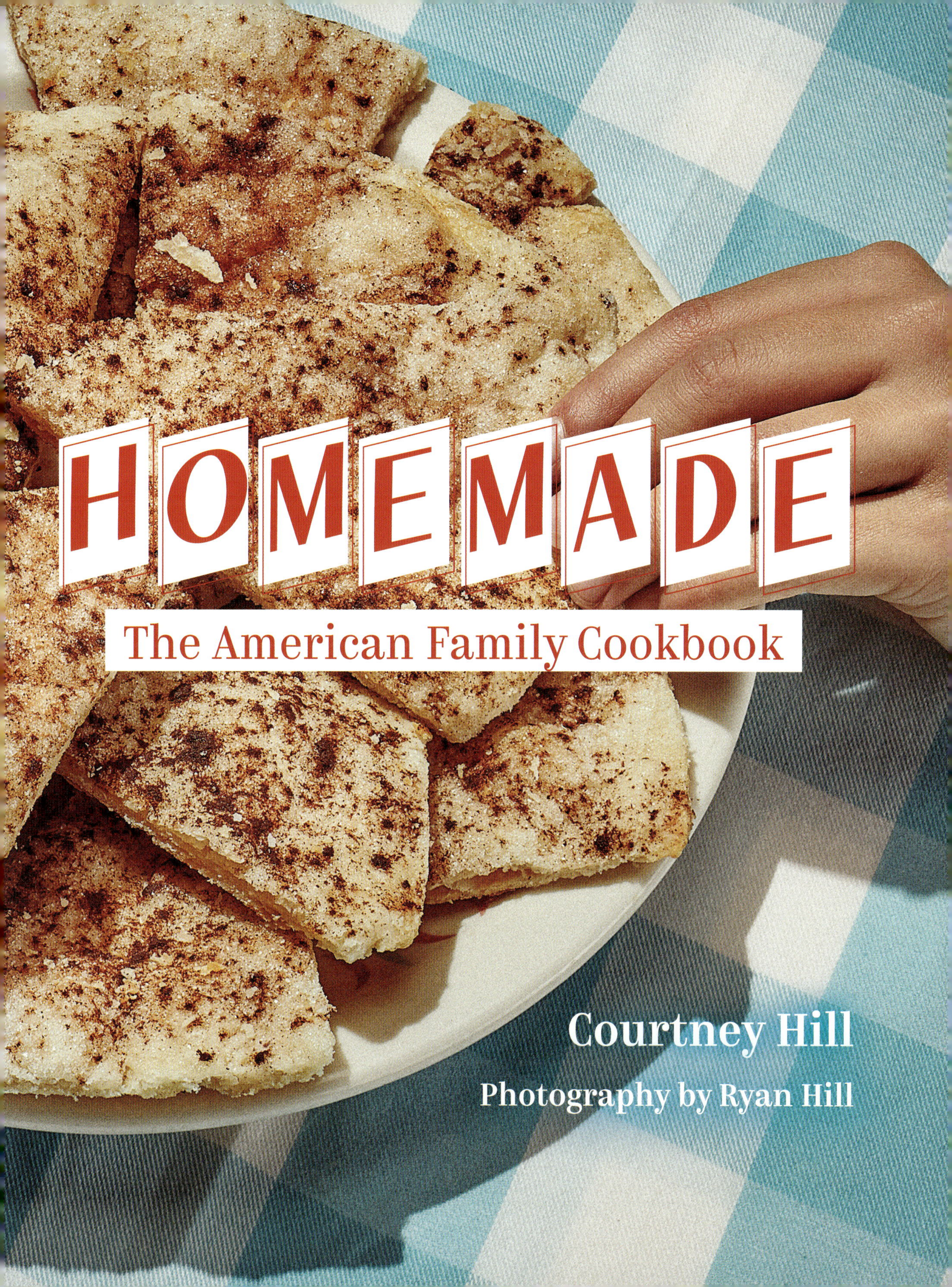
HOMEMADE
The American Family Cookbook
Courtney Hill
Photography by Ryan Hill

www.amplifypublishinggroup.com

HOMEMADE: THE AMERICAN FAMILY COOKBOOK

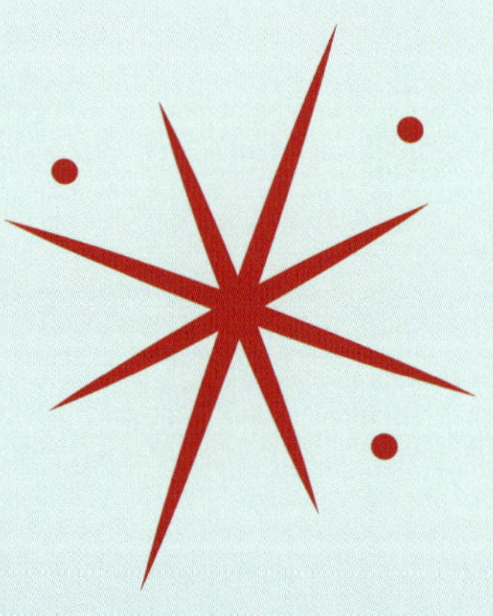

For more information, please contact:
Mascot Books, an imprint of Amplify Publishing Group
620 Herndon Parkway, Suite 320
Herndon, VA 20170
info@amplifypublishing.com

Library of Congress Control Number: 2021913790

CPSIA Code: PRQ0422A
ISBN-13: 978-1-63755-008-3

Printed in the United States

I dedicate this cookbook to my wonderful husband, Ryan. Without his love, support, and amazing talents, this dream would not have been realized. I love you, Ryan.

Recipes

Contents

Benchmark Breakfasts

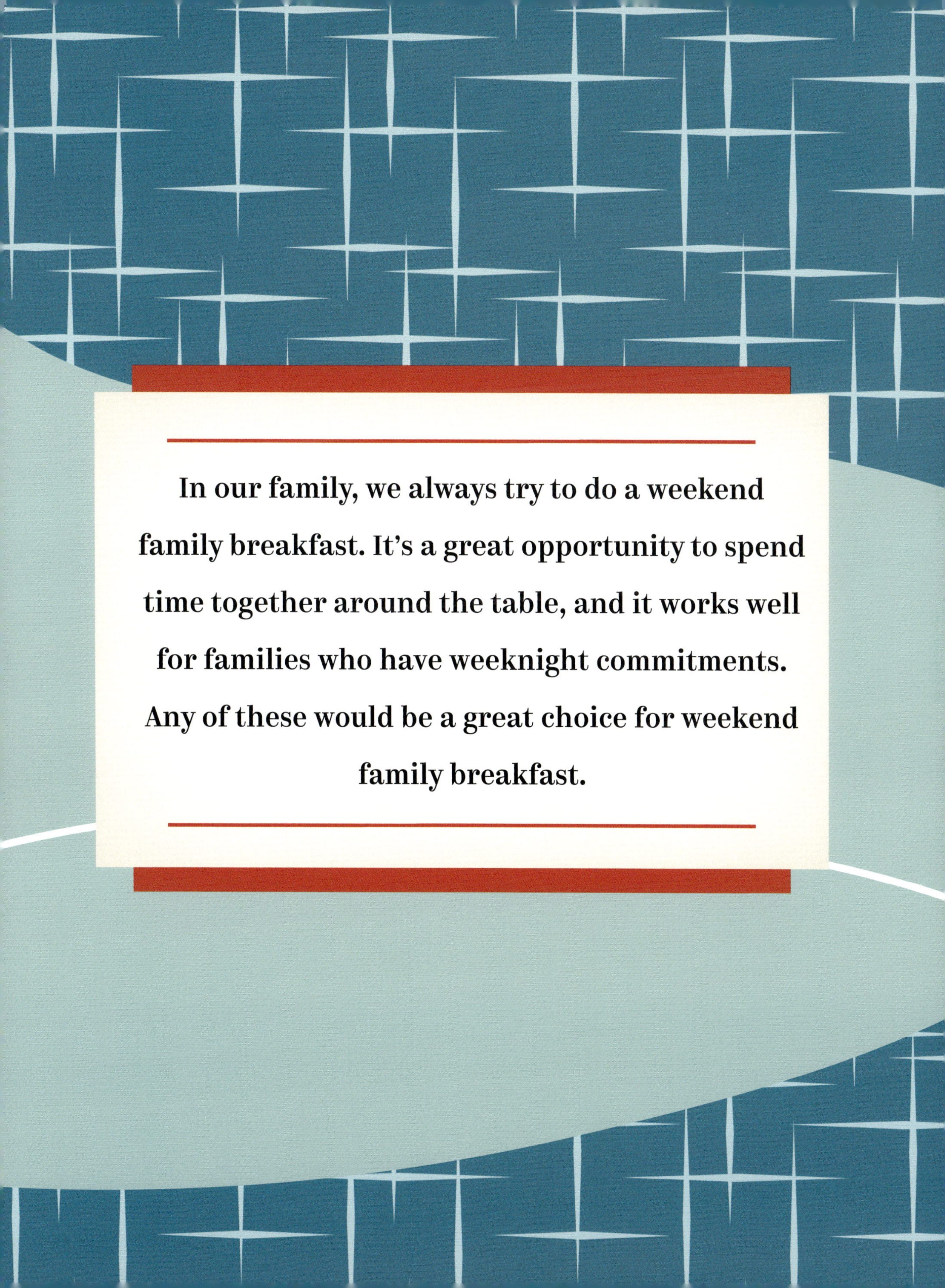

In our family, we always try to do a weekend family breakfast. It's a great opportunity to spend time together around the table, and it works well for families who have weeknight commitments. Any of these would be a great choice for weekend family breakfast.

Donut Holes

Refrigerator Biscuit Donut Holes

Ingredients

- 1 can refrigerated biscuits
- ½ cup sugar
- 1 tsp. cinnamon
- 2 cups frying oil

Directions

1. Cut each biscuits into 4ths.
2. Deep-fry until golden brown.
3. Drain on a paper towel.
4. Roll in cinnamon sugar.
5. Eat up and enjoy!

Apple Fritter Donut Holes (Variation)

Directions

1. Cut up 1 tart apple and sauté in butter until soft.
2. Add 2 tbs. sugar and allow the sugar to melt and coat the apples.
3. Pour apples over donut holes and toss.
4. Serve and enjoy!

Apple Pie Coffee Cake

Cake Batter Ingredients

- ¼ cup butter
- ¾ cup sugar
- 2 eggs
- ¾ cup oil
- ¼ cup yogurt or sour cream
- 1 tsp. vanilla
- ½ tsp. baking soda
- ½ tsp. baking powder
- ½ tsp. salt
- 1 tsp. cinnamon
- ¼ tsp. ginger
- ¼ tsp. nutmeg
- 1 ¾ cup flour
- 2 tart apples, diced

Cinnamon Swirl Ingredients

- ¾ cup brown sugar
- ⅓ cup flour
- ¼ cup cold butter, diced
- ½ tbs. cinnamon

Directions

1. Preheat oven to 350 degrees.
2. Cream together butter and sugar.
3. Add eggs, oil, yogurt, and vanilla. Mix well.

4. Add baking soda, baking powder, spices, and salt. Mix well.
5. Add flour. Mix well.
6. Peel, core, and dice apples.
7. In a separate bowl, combine the cinnamon-swirl ingredients until the butter is well incorporated.
8. Grease a 9x13 glass baking dish and spread ½ of the batter over the bottom.
9. Sprinkle ⅓ of the cinnamon-swirl mixture over the batter.
10. Spread the apples over the swirl evenly.
11. Sprinkle ⅓ more of the cinnamon-swirl mixture over the apples.
12. Spread the rest of the batter with a spatula.
13. Top with the remaining ⅓ of the swirl mixture.
14. Bake for 35–40 minutes, or until a toothpick comes out clean.

Banana Roll Ups

Ingredients

- 5–6 slices of bread
- 1–2 bananas, thinly sliced
- 1 egg
- 3 tbs. milk
- ½ tsp. of cinnamon
- ⅓ cup sugar

Did you know there are 2 types of brown sugar? One is sugar mixed with molasses, and the other—usually a bit more expensive—is actual brown sugar. Look at the ingredients on the back of the package to tell the difference.

Directions

1. Cut crusts off bread slices and roll slices, flat, with rolling pin.
2. Put 3 slices of banana at 1 end of the bread and roll it up.
3. In a shallow bowl, mix egg, milk, and 1/4 tsp. cinnamon. In another shallow bowl, mix sugar and remaining cinnamon.
4. Roll in the egg mixture, then in the sugar mixture.
5. Place in a nonstick skillet on medium heat. When sugar starts to bubble, flip and cook on the other side.
6. Plate up and enjoy! (Place the seam side down; otherwise it will stick to your plate.)

Homemade Whipped
Cream and Butter

Fresh Whipped Cream

Ingredients

- 2 cups heavy whipping cream
- ¼ cup or more of sugar

Directions

1. Pour heavy whipping cream into a stand-up mixer.
2. Attach the whisk attachment and whisk on high for several minutes until the liquid thickens into cream.
3. While it is whipping, add sugar.
4. Serve immediately or refrigerate for a few days.

Fresh Cream Butter

Ingredients

- 2 cups heavy whipping cream
- 1 tsp. salt

Directions

1. Pour heavy whipping cream into a stand-up mixer.
2. Attach the whisk and mix for 4–5 minutes. While mixing, add up to 1 tsp. of salt for salted butter.
3. Mix another 3–4 minutes until the butter bits form and liquid separates. The liquid is buttermilk.
4. Grab a handful of butter bits and squeeze out as much of the buttermilk as possible.
5. Repeat until you have retrieved as much of the butter as you can. Save the buttermilk if desired for other recipes.
6. Use right away or store in refrigerator.

Tip

Fresh whipped cream is wonderful in your morning coffee!

Cherry
Almond Scones

I've always thought scones were dry, hard, and tasteless. But these tender beauties are just the opposite!

Ingredients

- 2 cups flour
- 1 tbs. baking powder
- ¼ cup sugar
- ½ tsp. salt
- 6 tbs. cold butter, sliced
- ½ cup heavy whipping cream
- ½ cup milk
- 1 package of sweet dark cherries (canned or frozen, thawed)
- ¼ cup sliced almonds

Icing

- 1 tbs. butter
- 1 cup powdered sugar
- 1 tsp. salt
- ¼ tsp. almond extract
- Little bit of water

Directions

1. Sift together flour, baking powder, sugar, and 1 tsp. salt into a mixing bowl.
2. Add cold butter to the mixing bowl.
3. Using the paddle attachment, mix until the butter is incorporated into the dry ingredients—it will still be powdery.
4. Add cream and milk to the mixing bowl and mix until well combined.
5. Add the cherries and sliced almonds and mix a final time.
6. Spread a healthy amount of flour on your counter and turn out the dough.
7. Using more flour on top, lightly shape into a long rectangle.
8. Cut into triangles with a pizza cutter and place each triangle on a baking sheet lined with parchment paper.
9. Bake at 400 degrees for 18–22 minutes.
10. Allow scones to cool.
11. To make the icing, mix all ingredients in a bowl. Add little bits of water until desired consistency is reached. Drizzle over scones.
12. While the icing is still wet, sprinkle some sliced almonds on top of each scone.
13. Allow icing to solidify. To keep the icing picture perfect, add a little meringue powder, which turns the icing into royal icing and will keep its drizzle shape.
14. Serve and enjoy!

Sausage Breakfast Gravy

Ingredients

- ½ package of pork sausage
- 2 tbs. butter
- 2–4 tbs. flour
- 2 ½ cups milk
- salt and pepper to taste
- Your favorite biscuits

Directions

1. Brown sausage.
2. Put sausage in a small bowl and mix with 1–2 tbs. flour.
3. Melt butter in pan and add 1–2 tbs. flour. Mix to form a roux.
4. Add milk to pan and whisk.
5. Add salt and pepper to taste. When milk starts to steam, add sausage and whisk. Keep whisking until gravy has thickened.
6. Pour over biscuits and enjoy!

Homemade Biscuits

Ingredients

- 1 stick cold butter, diced
- 2 ½ cups flour
- 2 tbs. baking powder
- 1 tsp. salt
- 1 tsp. cream of tartar
- 1 cup milk and 1 tbs. lemon juice, or 1 cup buttermilk

Directions

1. In a mixing cup, add lemon juice to milk. Stir and let sit until used in the recipe.
2. Dice cold butter and place in a food processor.
3. Add the dry ingredients. Mix until butter is broken up and blended with flour.
4. Pour contents into a mixing bowl.
5. Add the milk mixture to the bowl and mix to combine.
6. Don't overwork the dough, but mix until it comes together to form a ball.
7. Roll out on a floured surface to about ¾ thickness.
8. Using a round cookie cutter or biscuit cutter, cut 12–13 biscuits from dough. Try to get all the cuts from the first roll; biscuits become tough if the dough is worked too much.
9. Place on a baking sheet. Make sure the biscuits are touching each other. This helps get a high rise.
10. Bake in a 375-degree oven for 15–17 minutes.

Cherry Chocolate Granola Bars

Ingredients

- ½ cup softened butter
- ½ cup honey or maple syrup
- ½ cup peanut butter
- 1 egg
- ½ cup packed brown sugar
- 1 tsp. vanilla extract
- ½ cup flour
- 4 ½ cups old-fashioned oats
- 1 tsp. baking soda
- dash of salt
- 1 cup chopped, dried cherries
- 1 cup mini chocolate chips

Directions

1. In a mixing bowl, mix butter, honey, and peanut butter.
2. Add egg, brown sugar, vanilla extract, and mix.
3. Add the baking soda, salt, and flour. Mix well.
4. Add oats and mix again.
5. Add dried cherries and mix.
6. Add mini chocolate chip and mix a final time.
7. Grease an oblong baking dish and turn out the dough. Flatten with a spatula.
8. Bake in a 325-degree oven for 15–20 minutes.
9. Allow to cool and cut into bars. Wrap each bar in plastic wrap.
10. Store in the refrigerator.

Blueberry Muffins

Blueberry Muffins

Here in the Midwest, we can grow just about anything. One of our favorite things to do as a family is to go fruit picking as each fruit comes into season. June is blueberry season. After picking, divide berries into quart-sized bags and freeze for later.

Ingredients

- ½ cup oil
- 1 egg
- ½ cup milk
- ¾ cup sugar
- 1 tsp. vanilla
- ½ tsp. salt
- 2 tsp. baking powder
- 1 ½ cups flour
- 1 cup fresh or frozen blueberries
- 1 orange or lemon

Streusel Topping

Ingredients

- ¼ cup butter
- ½ cup sugar
- ⅓ cup flour
- Zest of 1 orange or lemon

Directions

1. Preheat oven to 400 degrees.
2. Zest orange (or lemon) and set aside to be used in streusel.

3. Mix oil and egg. Add milk and juice of 1 orange and lemon and mix together with oil and egg.
4. Add sugar, vanilla, salt, and baking powder. Mix well.
5. Add flour and mix.
6. Fold in blueberries and fill muffin cups with ¼ cup batter.
7. Make streusel by mixing all ingredients in a bowl until butter is incorporated.
8. Evenly spoon streusel over muffins and bake for 20 minutes.
9. Let cool and enjoy!

Mixing oil and eggs first allows them to fully combine without over-mixing the batter. This method can be used in brownies, pancakes, etc. I'm calling it the Courtney Method.

Amazing Appetizers

Six-Layer Dip
Courtney's Hot Wings

Pinwheels

Six-Layer Bean Dip

This is a crowd favorite! We usually have it around Christmastime, but it's great for any occasion!

Ingredients

- 1 can Frito bean dip
- ¼ cup Miracle Whip
- ¼ sour cream
- ½ packet of taco seasoning
- 1 can of diced black olives
- 1–2 cups diced tomatoes (cherry and grape tomatoes work great for this)
- 1 bag of shredded lettuce
- 1–2 cups grated cheddar jack cheese

Directions

1. In a small bowl, mix together Miracle Whip, sour cream, and taco seasoning.
2. Start spreading out layers in a flat platter:
   a. bean dip
   b. taco seasoning
   c. diced olives
   d. diced tomatoes
   e. lettuce
   f. cheese
3. Serve with tortilla chips and watch it disappear!

Pinwheels

This is another classic hit at parties and showers.

Ingredients

- 1 package softened cream cheese
- 1 cup sour cream
- 1 can green chilies
- 1 can chopped black olives
- 1 cup grated cheddar cheese
- 2–3 chopped green onions
- 1 tsp. chili powder
- 1 tsp. salt
- 6–8 large tortillas

Directions

1. Mix together all the ingredients.
2. Spread a thin layer over each tortilla and roll up. Slice into 1-inch-thick slices and serve with salsa for dipping.

Fresh Veggie Pizza

This is one of my go-to recipes for showers and parties!

Ingredients

- 1 package refrigerator crescent rolls
- 1 package softened cream cheese
- ¼ cup Miracle Whip
- ¼ cup mayo
- ½ package powdered ranch dressing
- 1 cup grated cheddar cheese
- 1 cup chopped broccoli
- 1 cup diced yellow pepper
- 1 cup diced tomatoes (cherry or grape tomatoes work well for this)
- 1 cup shredded carrots
- 2 diced green onions, if desired

Directions

1. Roll out croissants flat on a cookie sheet.
2. Bake and let cool.
3. Mix mayo, Miracle Whip, cream cheese, and powdered ranch dressing in a bowl.
4. Spread out over croissants.
5. Spread out cheese and veggies.
6. Cut into squares or triangles, and place on a platter.

Salsa and Guacamole

Salsa

Ingredients

- 2 large tomatoes or 1 large can of tomatoes
- ½ yellow or orange bell pepper
- 1 jalapeño (leave out for mild; add for spicy)
- ¼ cup diced onion
- 1–2 tbs. chopped cilantro
- 2 tbs. lime juice

Directions

1. Place all ingredients in a food processor and pulse until you've reached desired consistency.
2. Serve with tortilla chips.

   (For those wanting extra spice, try adding a habanero pepper!)

Guacamole

Ingredients

- 3 ripe avocados
- 6 cherry or grape tomatoes
- ¼ cup diced onion
- 1 tbs. chopped cilantro
- 1 lime, juiced
- ½ tsp. salt

Directions

1. Place tomatoes, onions, cilantro, and lime juice in a bowl. Mix well and let stand for 15 minutes. This helps the guacamole not to turn brown as quickly.
2. Peel and mash avocados in a bowl.
3. Add the other ingredients and salt.
4. Mix well, adding more salt or lime juice if needed, and serve with tortilla chips.

How to choose a ripe avocado
Skin should be dark green and soft when squeezed. Remove the stem; it should be green underneath. If it's brown, it could be overripe. Unripe avocados are light green and very hard when squeezed.

Spa-Courtney
with Meat Sauce

Stuffed Mushrooms

Ingredients

- 12 button mushrooms
- 4 oz. softened cream cheese
- 2 tbs. Italian-style bread crumbs
- ½ tsp. salt
- ½ cup shredded mozzarella cheese
- 1 tbs. butter for brushing

Directions

1. Clean and destem the mushrooms. Place them on a foil-lined baking sheet.
2. In a bowl, mix together the cream cheese, bread crumbs, salt, and mozzarella cheese until well combined.
3. Fill each mushroom with cream cheese mixture.
4. Place under low broil for about 10 minutes, until brown, and you see some liquid at the bottom of each mushroom.
5. Brush each mushroom with butter and serve immediately.

Charcuterie and Crudités

This is one of my family's favorite busy weeknight meals. It can be pretty hearty, and it's very easy to prepare.

Charcuterie

1. Combine your favorite meats, cheeses, and fruits. You may also add nuts, olives, and pickles.

Crudités (cru-de-tay)

1. Cut various raw vegetables and arrange them on a platter.
2. Serve with dip (ranch or hummus).

Lip-Smacking Sammiches

Scrambled Egg
Sandwich

Scrambled Egg Sandwich

This sandwich is about as Midwest as you can get, and it celebrates garden fresh tomatoes.

Ingredients

- 1 garden-fresh tomato
- 3 eggs (for 2–3 sandwiches)
- 1–2 tbs. milk
- 1 tbs. butter
- salt and pepper to taste
- 1–2 tbs. Miracle Whip (per sandwich)
- 2 slices of bread (per sandwich)

Directions

1. Peel, slice, and salt a ripe tomato.
2. Crack eggs into a bowl with 1–2 tbs. of milk. Whisk.
3. Scramble eggs. Try to keep them in large pieces.
4. Assemble the sandwich as follows: 2 slices of bread, Miracle Whip, eggs, and tomato.
5. Serve while eggs are still warm.

Tomato-Growing Tips

I love to garden, and growing tomatoes is my absolute favorite! They are delicious just sliced with some salt. Growing up, we called these 'maters.

1. Here in the Midwest, I typically plant my seedlings around Mother's Day, when there is no danger of a hard overnight freeze. If a late freeze is coming, and you've already planted, cover them in plastic overnight to protect them.
2. As they begin to grow, look for the stems that grow in between 2 others. Those are called suckers, and you'll want to pick those off to help the overall health of your plants. When the tomatoes have grown, pick them at first blush (first sign of color) and let them finish ripening inside.
3. Be on the lookout for hornworms. They will devour your plants. They can be hard to spot because they blend in with the tomato plant so well. A telltale sign of them is eaten leaves or droppings.

Pearled Cous
Cous Salad

Turkey Surprise

If you are like me, you grew up eating a lot of turkey sandwiches. After a while they can get pretty boring. Here is a simple way to jazz it up!

Ingredients

- 2 slices of bread
- 4 slices of deli turkey
- 1 slice of cheddar cheese
- 1 tbs. mayo
- 1 tsp. mustard
- 1–2 tbs. Italian salad dressing
- lettuce and tomato

Directions

1. Cover a pan with foil and lay out your bread, cheese, and meat.
2. Place under the low broiler until the cheese melts.
3. Spread mayonnaise and mustard on the bread.
4. Cut into four sections and serve with Italian dressing for dipping.

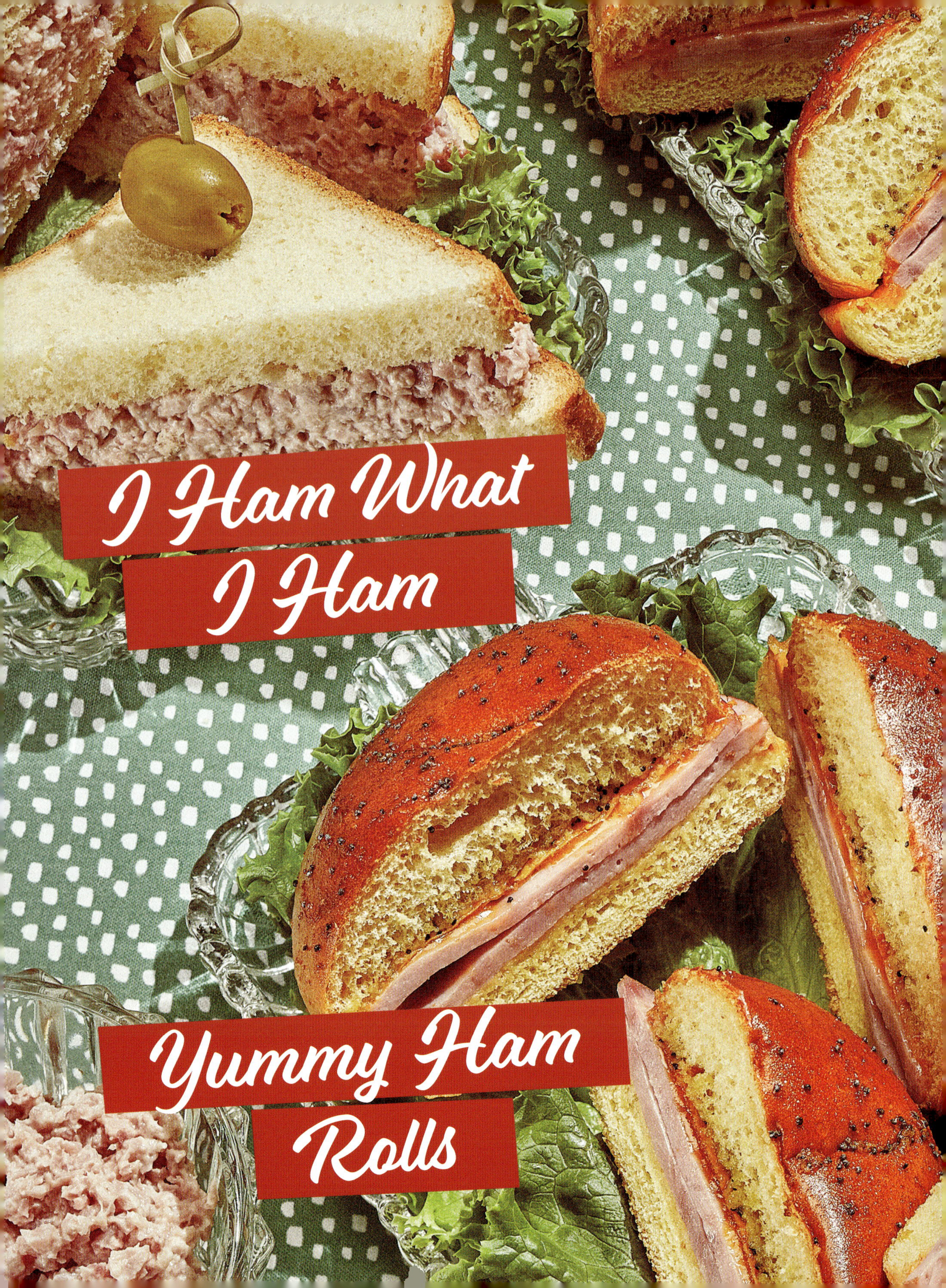
I Ham What
I Ham
Yummy Ham
Rolls

I Ham What I Ham Salad Sandwich

This recipe reminds me of Grandma Smith. She would get out her big meat grinder and grind up fresh ham for this classic Midwest sandwich. Such wonderful memories!

Ingredients

- 1–2 slices of ham (off the bone)
- ¼ cup Miracle Whip
- 2 slices of bread

Directions

1. Dice ham into cubes and pulse in a food processor until finely minced.
2. Add Miracle Whip and mix.
3. Serve between 2 slices of bread.

Yummy Ham Rolls

This one is another major crowd-pleaser—perfect to share while watching the big game!

Ingredients

- 12 rolls
- ½ cup melted butter
- 1 tbs. mustard
- 1 tbs. Worcestershire sauce
- ½ tsp. onion powder
- 1 tbs. poppy seeds

Directions

1. Preheat oven to 350 degrees.
2. Melt butter in the microwave in a glass bowl.
3. Add mustard, Worcestershire sauce, onion powder, and 1 tbs. poppy seeds. Stir to combine all ingredients.
4. Place the bottom sandwich rolls on a foil-lined baking sheet or a glass baking dish. Layer ham and cheddar cheese
5. Using a spoon or basting brush, brush some of the butter mixture on the underside of each top roll, and then place on sandwiches.
6. Brush the remaining butter mixture over the top of each sandwich.
7. Cover in foil and bake for 15 minutes.
8. Remove foil covering and bake for another 10 minutes.

All Grown-Up Grilled Cheese

Pairs nicely with the All Grown-Up Tomato Soup recipe listed on page 109.

Ingredients and Directions

1. Butter 1 side of a slice of sourdough bread.
2. Add a slice of smoked Gouda cheese.
3. Add a layer of cooked bacon (or bacon bits).
4. Add a layer of salted tomato slices.

5. Add another slice of cheese.
6. Top with another slice of buttered bread and grill until both sides of bread are browned, and the cheese is melted. Covering the sandwich with a lid can assist in melting the cheese.

Lettuce Eat Salad

Spinach Salad

Ingredients and Directions

1. Boil 2 eggs; peel and slice.
2. Slice 4–5 button mushrooms.
3. Wash and add 1 bag of spinach to a large bowl.
4. Add the egg, mushrooms, and 2 tbs. bacon bits.
5. Optional: caramelized onions add a great flavor as well.
6. Make dressing and pour over salad; toss and serve.

HOMEMADE

Dressing

- ⅓ cup oil
- ¼ cup red wine vinegar
- ¼ tsp. salt
- 1 tsp. sugar
- pinch of pepper

Image found on page 40

Pearled Couscous Salad

Ingredients and Directions

1. Make 1 cup pearled couscous according to package instructions, adding 1 tsp. basil while cooking.
2. Sauté 1 diced zucchini and ½ diced onion until tender.
3. Add to couscous and refrigerate until chilled.
4. Add 5–6 diced cherry tomatoes and ¼ cup Italian salad dressing, or more if needed.
5. Stir and serve chilled.

What the Kale? Salad

A kale salad that actually tastes good!

Ingredients and Directions

1. Rinse and remove kale leaves from center stem. Chop into bite-size pieces and add to bowl.
2. Rinse and chop romaine lettuce and add to bowl.
3. Add chopped broccoli, broccoli slaw, sliced almonds, sunflower seeds, and dried cranberries.

Dressing

- ¼ cup water
- ¼ cup white vinegar
- ¾ cup oil (vegetable or canola)
- 1 tsp. garlic powder
- 1 tsp. salt
- ¼ tsp. pepper

- 1 tsp. celery seed
- ½ tsp. celery salt
- ¼ tsp. onion powder
- ⅔ cup sugar
- 2 tsp. horseradish

Directions

1. Combine the following ingredients in a blender and blend for 30 seconds.
2. Pour desired amount over salad. Store the rest in the fridge.

Wilted Lettuce
Salad

This is another Midwest classic. It is so delicious with fresh garden lettuce—the perfect complement to a BLT!

Ingredients and Directions

1. In a skillet, melt 3–4 tbs. bacon grease.
2. Sauté 2–3 tbs. chopped red onion in the grease until tender.
3. Stir in ⅓ cup sugar and ⅓ cup white vinegar until sugar is dissolved.
4. Let cool slightly and pour desired amount over baby salad greens.

Easy Vinaigrette Salad Dressings

Forget the added ingredients and preservatives of store-bought vinaigrettes. These simple dressings taste amazing and are so easy to make.

Ingredients and Directions (1 serving; multiply for larger salads)

White Vinaigrette

1. Combine the following ingredients in a jar and shake until incorporated:
    - 1 tbs. honey
    - 2 tbs. white wine vinegar
    - 3 tbs. oil (grape seed, olive, or vegetable)
    - salt and pepper to taste

Red Wine Vinaigrette

- 1 tbs. honey
- 2 tbs. red wine vinegar
- 3 tbs. oil (grape seed, olive, or vegetable)
- salt and pepper to taste

Creamy Vinaigrette

- 1 tbs. honey
- 2 tbs. white wine vinegar
- 3 tbs. mayo
- salt and pepper to taste
- Make sure to continue to mix until completely smooth.

Fruit Vinaigrette

- 2 tbs. fruit jam (strawberry, peach, raspberry, etc.)
- 3 tbs. oil
- 2 tbs. vinegar
- salt and pepper to taste

The Main
Event

Classic Beef
Roast

Classic Beef Roast Dinner with Gravy

I love roasts because they are so simple and delicious, and all your sides are included!

Ingredients

- preferred beef roast cut (bone-in will be more tender and moist)
- salt and pepper
- several carrots
- several potatoes
- 1 onion
- 1 cup water
- 2 beef bouillon cubes
- 1 tsp. Kitchen Bouquet
- 2 tbs. cornstarch

Searing the roast on all sides seals in moisture and adds great flavor.

Directions

1. Preheat oven to 275 degrees.
2. Peel and cut carrots, potatoes, and onions.
3. Put some oil into a Dutch oven or skillet, and turn heat to medium high.
4. Put salt and pepper on the roast and rub into the meat.
5. Sear both sides of the roast for a couple of minutes.

6. Add bouillon cubes and 1–2 cups of water, depending on size of the roast.
7. Cover and place in oven for 3 hours. Add vegetables after 1 hour.
8. Halfway through, check to make sure you have enough liquid. Add more water if needed. When it's finished, transfer meat and vegetables to a platter. Use dripping to make gravy.
9. This could easily be cooked in a Crockpot. Just make sure to sear your meat and then cook low and slow all day. I'd put only 1 cup of water if cooking in the Crockpot.

Brown Gravy

1. Transfer your drippings to a skillet.
2. Remove a small amount of the hot liquid and mix together with a couple of tbs. of cornstarch. Add mixture back into the skillet and stir.
3. Add 1 tsp. Kitchen Bouquet. Gravy will boil and thicken.
4. Pour over your roast and veggies. Serve with bread and butter, and enjoy!

Roast Chicken Dinner with Gravy

Ingredients and Directions

1. You can use whatever cut of bone-in, skin-on chicken you like. Sprinkle with salt and place in your Dutch oven.
2. Peel and cut your vegetables (carrots, potatoes, and onion) into smaller pieces.
3. Add 1 cup of water and 1 chicken bouillon cube, and place Dutch oven in a 275-degree oven for 1 ½–2 hours.
4. Transfer the meat and vegetables to a platter, and transfer the liquid to a skillet.
5. To make the gravy, remove a small amount of the hot liquid into a cup and add 1 tbs. cornstarch. Mix together and stir back into your skillet.
6. Allow gravy to boil and thicken.
7. Plate it up and serve with a piece of bread and butter. Add ½ tsp. of Kitchen Bouquet to give your gravy a rich, dark color.
8. Enjoy!

Finger-Lickin' Fried Chicken with Gravy

This is one of my all-time favorite recipes! I make it at least once every other week!

Ingredients and Directions

1. Thaw chicken breasts; butterfly and cut into smaller pieces.
2. Flour chicken pieces in ½ cup flour mixed with ½ tbs. seasoned salt.
3. Dip pieces in milk, then back in the flour.
4. Place the pieces in a frying pan with ¼ in oil heated to medium heat.
5. Leave pieces undisturbed for several minutes.
6. Turn pieces when bottom edges turn golden brown.
7. Fry on the other side for the same amount of time.
8. Remove chicken pieces and place on a paper towel to absorb extra oil.

Double-dipping chicken pieces creates a crispier crust.

White Gravy

1. Add 1–2 tbs. flour to the oil in the pan and stir to make a roux.
2. Add 2 ½ cups milk and whisk.
3. When bubbles occur, add salt, pepper, and chicken bouillon crumbles to taste.
4. Allow to boil until desired thickness is reached.

Chicken-Fried Steak

Ingredients and Direction

1. Use a tenderized cut of steak (such as cubed steak).
2. Flour steak pieces in ½ cup flour mixed with ½ tbs. seasoned salt. This is known as dredging.
3. Dip pieces in milk, then back in the flour.
4. Place the pieces in a frying pan with ¼ in oil heated to medium heat.
5. Leave pieces undisturbed for several minutes.
6. Turn pieces when bottom edges turn golden brown.
7. Fry on the other side for the same amount of time. (There may be some blood, and that's okay. Steak can be eaten in various rare forms.)
8. Remove steak pieces and place on a paper towel to absorb extra oil.
9. Use the same recipe for the gravy, but use a beef bouillon cube instead of a chicken one.

Courtney's Hot Wings

Image found on page 22

Ingredients

- 20 chicken wings
- flour and seasoned salt for dredging
- oil for frying
- ¼ cup butter
- 1 cup Louisiana hot sauce
- 2 tbs. honey

Deep-fry outside to avoid stinking up your house.

Directions

1. Fill deep fryer to max fill line with canola, vegetable, or peanut oil, and turn heat to 375 degrees.
2. In a large bowl, combine flour and seasoned salt.
3. Add wings and coat with flour or dredge.
4. In a saucepan, add butter, hot sauce, and honey. Turn the heat to medium, and stir until butter is melted and sauce is combined. Turn heat to low to keep warm while wings are frying.

5. When the oil is hot, add wings. Fry in shifts of 6–8 wings of similar size.
6. The wings are done when they float to the top and turn golden brown.
7. Remove wings and drain on a paper towel.
8. Coat in sauce.
9. Serve immediately with celery and ranch or blue cheese dressing.

Chicken and Tomatoes

This is a recipe my mom fixed a lot when I was growing up. Now it's a favorite of my kids as well!

Ingredients

- 6 bone-in, skin-on chicken thighs (or other cut of chicken meat)
- butter and seasoned salt
- 1 package dry onion soup mix
- 2 cups water
- 2 cans diced tomatoes
- 1 tsp. basil
- rice or cauliflower rice

Directions

1. Using your choice of bone-in, skin-on chicken, place in a glass baking dish. Dot with butter and sprinkle with seasoned salt. Bake at 425 degrees for 30 minutes or until the internal temp reaches 165 degrees.
2. Remove the skin and remove the bones. Dice chicken.
3. In a Dutch oven or stockpot, add dry onion soup mix and water.
4. Add canned tomatoes, basil, and diced chicken.
5. Cover and simmer for about 45 minutes or until the liquid reduces to form a stew consistency.
6. Serve over rice or cauliflower rice.

For a healthy alternative, use cauliflower rice instead of white rice. Add a chicken bouillon cube and some seasoned salt to enhance the flavor before topping with the chicken and tomatoes.

Swiss Steak

Ingredients

- 1 lb. or more of round steak
- salt and pepper
- flour for dredging
- 1 medium onion, sliced
- 2 bell peppers, sliced
- 2 jars of canned tomatoes

Directions

1. Cut round steak into a portion-size piece. Add salt and pepper on each side.
2. Dredge in flour and brown for a couple of minutes on each side in hot oil.
3. In a Crockpot, layer steak, peppers, onions, and tomatoes until all ingredients are in the pot. Add salt and pepper to taste.
4. Allow to cook for 6–8 hours.
5. Serve over mashed potatoes.

Mini Meat Loaves

Image found on page 97

This is a kid-pleaser with veggies hidden inside. Don't tell the kids!

Ingredients

- 1–2 shredded carrots
- ½ small onion, finely chopped
- ½ lb. ground beef
- 1 egg, beaten
- ketchup
- 2 tbs. bread crumbs
- 1–2 tbs. Worcestershire sauce
- ½ tsp. salt
- ½ cup finely chopped spinach

Directions

1. Preheat oven to 350 degrees. I like to put the carrots and spinach in a food processor.
2. In a skillet, sauté carrots and onion until soft.
3. Add spinach and cook down.
4. In a bowl, combine ground beef, egg, bread crumbs, Worcestershire sauce, salt, and veggie mix.
5. Mix together all ingredients and form patties.
6. Place patties in a glass baking dish and bake for 15 minutes.
7. Turn patties and squirt each with ketchup. Bake for 15 additional minutes. To help grease drain, bake on top of a cooling rack placed on a baking sheet. Grease will drain below the patties.

Creamy Chicken Enchiladas

Ingredients

- 2–3 boneless skinless chicken breasts
- ½ stick butter
- 1 cup mushrooms, sliced
- ¼ cup onion, diced
- 1 red bell pepper, chopped
- 1 can cream of chicken soup
- 2 cups sour cream
- 1 tbs. chili powder
- 1 package of dry enchilada seasoning
- 1 can tomato sauce
- 8 large tortillas
- 2 cups grated cheddar cheese

Directions

1. Boil chicken breasts in water with seasoned salt and chili powder for 10 minutes, or until tender. Allow to cool and chop.
2. Sauté in butter, sliced mushrooms, and onion until tender. Set aside.
3. Sauté chopped red sweet peppers until tender.
4. In a mixing bowl, combine soup, sour cream, 1 tbs. chili powder, onions, mushrooms, and chopped chicken.
5. Mix package of enchilada seasoning mix with tomato sauce and 1 can of water.
6. Coat 8 large tortillas in sauce. Spoon in chicken mixture. Roll and place in a 9x13 glass baking dish.
7. Pour remaining sauce over rolled tortilla.
8. Top with grated cheddar cheese and bake for 30 minutes at 350 degrees.

Seared Steak with Leek
Mushroom Cream Sauce

This one is for when you are feeling fancy or cooking for someone you want to impress! I recommend using a filet or sirloin steak for this.

Directions

1. Salt and pepper each side of the steak.
2. Melt 3–4 tbs. butter in a skillet over medium-high heat. Sear the steaks for 2 minutes on each side.
3. Place a wire rack on a baking sheet and put the steaks on top. Finish them off in a 400-degree oven for 8 minutes. This gives you a nice medium-rare steak, depending on the thickness. If you like it well done, sear and bake for a few more minutes.
4. Allow the steaks to rest for at least 10 minutes before cutting into them to keep the juices in.

Leek Mushroom Cream Sauce

Ingredients

- 5–6 button mushrooms, sliced
- 1 leek, sliced

Basic White Sauce

Ingredients

- 2 tbs. butter
- 2 tbs. flour
- 1 cup milk
- ½ tsp. salt

Directions

1. Sauté mushrooms and leeks in 2 tbs. butter over medium heat until soft, then set aside.
2. In a saucepan, melt 2 tbs. butter and stir in flour to form a roux. Let the roux cook for 1 minute or so to remove any floury taste.
3. Add milk, salt, and stir. Allow it to thicken. Add the mushrooms and leeks, and allow sauce to thicken a little more.
4. Top your steak and enjoy!

If you have leftover sauce, it is really good over egg noodles! Just add a beef bouillon cube and water or some beef broth to thin out the sauce and serve over cooked egg noodles.

Cur-azy Good Chicken Casserole

This is another recipe from my childhood. So good!

Ingredients

- 2–4 chicken breasts
- 2 crowns broccoli (can use frozen; just thaw before you use)
- 1 can cream of chicken soup
- ¼ cup mayo
- ¼ cup Miracle Whip
- ½ tsp. yellow curry powder
- french-fried onions

Directions

1. Cook and chop chicken. You can boil or bake, or you can use a rotisserie chicken.
2. Cut into bite-size pieces and cook broccoli (boil or steam).
3. In a mixing bowl, add soup, mayo, Miracle Whip, and curry. Mix together.
4. Add chopped chicken and chopped broccoli. Mix together.
5. Spread into an oblong baking dish and bake at 350 for 10 minutes.
6. Sprinkle french-fried onions all over the top and bake for another 10 minutes.
7. Enjoy!

Pork-n-Pineapple
Tacos

Ingredients

- 1 pork tenderloin
- 1 can tomato paste
- ½ cup tomato juice
- 1 6-oz. can pineapple juice
- 1 tbs. brown sugar
- 1 tsp. cumin
- 1 tbs. chili powder
- 1 onion, cut into quarters
- salt and pepper
- tortilla and other fixings, such as shredded red cabbage, cheese, sour cream, and pineapple salsa

Directions

1. Place pork tenderloin in a slow cooker and sprinkle generously with salt and pepper.
2. In a mixing bowl, combine tomato paste, tomato juice, pineapple juice, brown sugar, cumin, and chili powder.
3. Pour over tenderloin and add onion.
4. Let cook for 6 hours.
5. Remove pork and shred with a fork.
6. Discard the onion and add pork back to the sauce until serving.

Pineapple Salsa

Ingredients

- 1 jalapeño or mini sweet pepper (according to preference), finely chopped
- 1 slice of onion, finely chopped
- 1 tbs. cilantro, minced
- ½ cup pineapple chunks, chopped
- lime juice and salt to taste

Directions

1. Combine and chill until serving.

To get the onion smell off your hands, wash them with dish soap while rubbing them around a stainless steel spoon. It works—try it!

Plum Good Chicken

This recipe is just plum good!

Ingredients

- 6–8 bone-in, skin-on chicken thighs
- ½ cup plum jam
- ½ cup soy sauce
- 1 tbs. grated ginger
- 1 tbs. honey
- ½ diced red onion or 2 sliced green onions
- 1 tbs. corn starch

Directions

1. Preheat oven to 425 degrees.
2. Place thighs in a glass baking dish.

3. In a mixing bowl, mix jam, soy sauce, ginger, and honey until relatively incorporated.
4. Pour sauce over thighs and sprinkle with onions.
5. Bake at 425 degrees for 30 minutes.
6. Remove from oven and pour sauce into a skillet. Place chicken back in oven to finish cooking—until juices run clear and internal temperature reaches 165 degrees.
7. Add cornstarch to sauce and whisk until smooth. Bring to a boil and let thicken. Remove from heat and pour into a serving dish.
8. Place thighs on a serving dish and pour a little sauce over each.
9. Serve with cooked veggies and rice. For best Asian rice, add 1–2 tbs. rice wine vinegar after it has cooked.
10. The sauce is great on the veggies and rice as well.

Pasta la Vista, Baby!

Spa-Courtney with Meat Sauce

Image found on page 28

This recipe is a great way to jazz up a store-bought sauce (or make the homemade sauce). It sneaks in some vegetables without changing the flavor of the sauce.

Ingredients

- 1 lb. spaghetti pasta
- 1 small zucchini, chopped
- 1 jar canned tomatoes, diced
- ¼ onion, minced
- ½ lb. ground beef
- ½ tsp. garlic powder
- ½ tsp. onion powder
- salt and pepper to taste
- 1 jar of your favorite pasta sauce
- 1–2 tbs. oil

Directions

1. Cook pasta to al dente.
2. In a skillet, heat the oil over medium heat. Add minced onion and chopped zucchini, and sauté until tender (light brown surface) and set aside
3. Brown the ground beef in the skillet and drain the fat into a container. Allow fat to cool and harden, then discard in the trash. Add the garlic powder, onion powder, and season with salt and pepper.
4. Add the zucchini, onions, and canned tomatoes. Allow to simmer 1–2 minutes.
5. Add the pasta sauce and simmer for 10 minutes.
6. Pour over your pasta and serve with grated Parmesan cheese.

How to drain excess grease from ground beef: Tilt the pan down, push the meat up, and spoon out the grease into a bowl. Let harden and discard.

GG's Homemade Pasta Sauce

This is Grandma Gibson's basic red sauce recipe, with a few minor changes.

Directions

1. Place the following ingredients in a saucepan and allow to simmer for 10 min.

Ingredients

- 1 tsp. onion powder
- 1 tbs. sugar
- ¼ tsp. pepper
- ½ tsp. salt
- 1 tsp. oregano
- 1 tsp. basil
- 1 bay leaf (remove for serving)
- ½ tsp. garlic powder
- 1 can diced tomatoes
- 1 can tomato paste
- 1 can water
- 1 can crushed tomatoes
- 1 can tomato sauce

Low-carb option –roasted spaghetti squash instead of pasta.

Cut spaghetti squash in half and remove seeds. Place both halves in a glass baking dish. Drizzle with oil and sprinkle with salt, pepper, and garlic salt. Roast at 400 until tender. Use a fork to scrape the squash out; it will be stringy like spaghetti pasta.

Spinach Artichoke Casserole

Cubed cooked chicken breast can be added if desired! This recipe is a major crowd-pleaser!

Ingredients

- 1 lb. penne pasta
- 2–4 tbs. oil
- ½ onion, minced
- 1 clove garlic
- 1 stick plus 2 tbs. butter
- 2 tbs. flour
- 2 cup milk
- 1 cup water
- 2 tsp. salt
- 4 oz. soften cream cheese, cubed
- 1 cup Parmesan cheese
- 2 cup shredded mozzarella cheese
- 1 cup sour cream
- ¼ cup mayo
- ¼ cup Miracle Whip
- 1 tsp. red pepper flakes (optional for a kick)
- 1 jar artichoke hearts, chopped
- 1 bag fresh spinach, chopped
- 1 package Ritz cracker

Directions

1. Cook pasta to al dente and set aside.
2. Preheat oven to 350 degrees.
3. Place 1–2 tbs. oil in a skillet over medium heat. Add the onion and sauté until tender. Add garlic clove.
4. Add the bag of spinach and sauté until cooked. Set aside. Remove and discard garlic clove.
5. In a saucepan over medium heat, make a basic white sauce. Melt 2 tbs. butter. Add 2 tbs. flour and mix to form a roux. Add milk, water, and salt. Bring to a simmer while stirring.
6. Add cream cheese, mozzarella cheese, sour cream, mayo, and Miracle Whip until melted and well combined; set aside.
7. In a 9x13 glass baking dish, combine sauce, artichokes, spinach, and onions, then stir in pasta. Add cooked chicken if desired.
8. Crush crackers and sprinkle over casserole.
9. Melt butter and drizzle over casserole.
10. Bake for 30 minutes.

Classic Mac
BBQ Mac

Homemade Mac and Cheese

Classic

Great side dish or entrée!

Ingredients

- 1 lb. macaroni pasta
- 1 stick butter
- 2 ½ cup shredded cheddar cheese
- 1 can condensed cheddar cheese soup
- 1 cup milk
- ½ cup sour cream
- ½ tsp. dry mustard
- ½ tsp. salt
- ¼ tsp. pepper
- 1 package crushed Ritz crackers

Directions

1. Preheat oven to 350 degrees.
2. Cook macaroni to al dente and set aside.
3. In a saucepan, melt ½ stick butter. Add the cheddar cheese and stir until melted and gooey.
4. Add cheese soup, milk, sour cream, dry mustard, salt, and pepper. Stir until well combined.
5. Place pasta in a 9x13 baking dish and pour on sauce. Stir to combine.
6. Sprinkle with crushed crackers. Melt butter and drizzle over the top.
7. Bake for 30 minutes. Sometimes I don't want to make as much, so I only use half the sauce. I freeze the other half, and it's ready for when I want to make it again.

BBQ Chicken Mac and Cheese

Mac and cheese as a main dish!

Directions

1. Using a whole smoked chicken, remove the skin. Remove the meat from the bones and chop.
2. Combine the meat with your favorite BBQ sauce and stir into the classic mac and cheese recipe. Top with butter and crackers, then bake.

Tuscan Chicken Pasta

A meal in a skillet!

Ingredients

- ½ lb. corkscrew pasta
- ½ cup sun-dried tomatoes with oil
- ½ lb. boneless, skinless chicken breast, butterflied and cut into large nuggets
- flour
- seasoned salt
- 1 cup milk
- 4 oz. softened cream cheese, diced into cubes
- ½ cup shredded mozzarella cheese
- ½ cup shredded cheddar cheese
- ½ tsp. salt
- ½ tsp. basil

Directions

1. Cook pasta to al dente in salted water. Save water.
2. In a skillet over medium heat, place tomatoes and oil. Sauté the tomatoes until lightly browned. Remove and set aside.
3. Mix some flour and seasoned salt in a shallow bowl, and dredge each chicken piece. Fry chicken in hot tomato oil, adding more if the chicken starts to stick, on each side until cooked all the way through.
4. Add milk, cheeses, and cream cheese. Stir until melted together into a creamy sauce.
5. Chop the sun-dried tomatoes and add to the skillet with the basil and salt.
6. Combine sauce with chicken and pasta (add some pasta water if sauce is too thick).

Chicken Tetrazzini

This is my go-to hospitality meal! When I'm taking a meal to a friend or church member, this is a great option. It's a delicious dish for any palate.

Ingredients

- 3-4 cups rotisserie chicken, chopped
- seasoned salt
- 1 lb. spaghetti pasta
- 2 cups milk
- ½ tsp. salt
- ¾ cup butter
- ¼ cup flour
- ½ cup sour cream
- 1 can cream of mushroom soup
- 1 can cream of chicken soup
- 1 lb. Velveeta cheese
- 8–10 sliced mushrooms
- 1 medium zucchini, diced
- ½ onion minced
- 1 medium yellow squash, diced

Directions

1. Cook pasta and set aside.
2. In a skillet over medium heat, melt 2 tbs. butter and sauté onions until tender.
3. Add mushrooms and sauté until tender. Remove and set aside.
4. Add 2 tbs. butter to the skillet and sauté zucchini and squash until lightly browned and tender. Add to the onions and mushrooms. Set aside.
5. In a saucepan over medium heat, melt 1/4 cup butter. Add flour and stir to form a roux. Add milk, salt, and cubed Velveeta cheese. Stir until melted. Add sour cream, the 2 soups, and a half cup of the pasta water (to thin out the sauce). Stir until well combined.
6. Mix together with pasta, chicken, and vegetables in a 9x13 glass baking dish.
7. Bake for 30 minutes.

Lasagna Pasta

I find regular lasagna a little hard to eat and reheat. This dish has all the taste of lasagna, but it's much easier to eat, freeze, and reheat.

Sauce Layer Ingredients

- 1 lb. ground beef
- 1 tsp. garlic powder
- 1 tsp. onion powder
- 1 tsp. basil
- 1 tsp. oregano
- 16 oz. tomato juice
- 8 oz. tomato sauce
- 12 oz. tomato paste
- 1 tsp. salt

Cottage Cheese Layer

- 3 cups small curd cottage cheese
- ½ cup Parmesan cheese
- 1 tbs. parsley
- 2 eggs, beaten
- ½ tsp. garlic salt
- ½ tsp. pepper

Other Ingredients

- 2 lbs. penne pasta
- 3 cups shredded mozzarella
- cheese

Directions

1. Preheat oven to 350 degrees.
2. Cook pasta and set aside.
3. In a skillet over medium heat, brown ground beef, discarding the fat.
4. In the skillet, add garlic powder, onion powder, basil, oregano, tomato juice, tomato paste, tomato sauce, and crushed tomatoes. Simmer for 10 minutes.
5. In a bowl, combine beaten eggs, cottage cheese, Parmesan cheese, parsley, garlic, salt, and pepper.
6. In a 9x13 pan, place a layer of pasta, cottage cheese mixture, sauce, and mozzarella cheese. Repeat until all ingredients are used. Typically yields 2 complete layers.
7. Bake for 30 minutes.

The Sideshow

German Coleslaw

This is a copycat recipe from one of my favorite hometown restaurants. It is a must-have with the fried chicken recipe.

Ingredients and Directions

1. Shred ½ head of cabbage.
2. Mix the following together in a lidded container: ¼ tsp. garlic powder, 1 tsp. salt, ½ tsp. pepper, 6 tbs. oil, and ¼ cup white vinegar.
3. Pour dressing over slaw and toss.
4. Chill slaw for several hours before serving.

Country-Style Green Beans

It is an important Midwest kitchen rule to never throw out bacon grease. I save it in a jar in the fridge and add it to various recipes, such as this one!

Ingredients

- 1 lb. of green beans
- ¼ red onion, chopped
- 1–2 tbs. bacon grease
- 1–1 ½ tsp. salt
- bacon bits
- water

Directions

1. Clean green beans and break off the ends.
2. Put them in a stockpot with chopped red onion, bacon bits, bacon grease, and salt.
3. Add enough water to cover the bottom of the pan (½ cup or so). Boil until soft (20–30 minutes).
4. Drain water and more salt to taste.

Baked Beans

Mini
Meat Loaves
Glazed Rainbow
Carrots

Baked Beans

What's a BBQ without baked bean? This is my mom's recipe, and it's the best baked beans recipe ever (very good alongside the mini meat loaves)!

Ingredients

- 1 large or 2 small cans Pork-n-Beans
- ½ cup ketchup
- 1 tbs. mustard
- ½ cup brown sugar
- 1-2 tbs. Worcestershire sauce
- 2–3 strips of cooked bacon (crumbled)
- ¼ cup diced onion

Directions

1. Combine all ingredients and pour into a square glass baking dish. Bake for 30 minutes at 350 degrees.

Fried Potatoes

Another classic Midwest side dish—simple and delicious!

Ingredients

- 4 medium potatoes
- ½ onion, diced
- 2-3 tbs. oil
- 1 tbs. butter
- Salt

Directions

1. Peel and thinly slice potatoes.
2. Heat oil in a nonstick skillet.
3. Add potatoes, onions, butter and salt.
4. Panfry until potatoes are tender. Turn up heat slightly to brown the potatoes to desired crispness.

Glazed Rainbow Carrots

The colors in this side dish are great, but, of course, if you can't find rainbow carrots, regular orange carrots will work wonderfully.

Ingredients

- 1 lb sliced rainbow carrots
- water
- 2 tbs. butter
- ½ tsp salt
- 1 tbs. sugar

Directions

1. Peel and evenly slice carrots.
2. Place in a skillet and pour on just enough water to cover the carrots.
3. Add butter, salt, and sugar.
4. Turn heat to medium and allow carrots to simmer until all the liquid is gone leaving a glaze. Stir to coat and serve.

Basic Cheese Sauce

Great over cooked veggies!

Ingredients

- 2 tbs. butter
- 2 tbs. flour
- 1 cup milk
- ½ tsp. salt
- 6 oz. Velveeta Cheese, cubed

Directions

1. In a saucepan, melt 2 tbs. butter and stir in flour to form a roux. Let the roux cook for 1 minute or so to remove any floury taste.
2. Add milk and salt. Stir until mixed together. Allow it to thicken.
3. Add cheese cubes. Stir until melted and creamy.

Cheesy Green Beans

Even better than green bean casserole! Give it a try!

Ingredients

- 1 serving basic cheese sauce (see previous recipe)
- 4 cans or 2 bags frozen French-cut green beans
- ¼ tsp. chili powder
- fried onions straws

Directions

1. Preheat oven to 350 degrees.
2. Cook 1 large bag of French-cut frozen green beans, according to the package instructions, and place in a glass baking dish.
3. In a saucepan, combine flour and butter over medium heat until smooth to create a roux.
4. Add milk and salt. Stir to combine.
5. Add Velveeta cheese and stir until the cheese has melted, and the sauce has become thick and creamy.
6. Stir in chili powder.
7. Pour the cheese sauce over the beans and stir to combine. Put into a glass baking dish.
8. Sprinkle with french-fried onions and top with foil.
9. Bake for 15 minutes. Remove foil and bake for an additional 15 minutes.

Roasted Marinated Veggies

This is my favorite way to roast veggies.

Ingredients

- 1 zucchini, sliced
- 1 package button mushrooms
- 1 onion, chopped
- 1 pepper, chopped

Directions

1. Place all veggies in a bowl. Add 2–3 tbs. each of Italian dressing, soy sauce, and Worcestershire sauce. Toss until mixed well.
2. Marinate for a few hours.
3. Pour out on a foil-lined pan and roast at 425 degrees until tender.

This marinade is wonderful on steaks and chicken.

Soup! There It Is

Broccoli Cheese
Soup

Broccoli Cheese Soup

Goes so well in a bread bowl with a slice of sourdough bread for dipping!

Ingredients

- 3 stalks of celery
- ½ onion
- ¼ cup butter
- 1 carton chicken broth or stock
- 2 bunches of broccoli heads (or 1 bag frozen broccoli)
- 1 cup milk
- 1 cup half-and-half
- 16 oz. Velveeta cheese
- ¼ cup flour

Directions

1. Finely chop celery and an onion. Sauté in the bottom of a Dutch oven or stockpot in butter until tender (5–10 minutes) over medium heat.
2. Steam broccoli until tender.
3. Add flour to the celery and onions. Cook for 1–2 minutes.
4. Add chicken broth and broccoli. Cover and cook for another 10 minutes.
5. Add 1 cup of milk and 1 cup of half-and-half.
6. Cut Velveeta cheese into small cubes and add to the pot. Stir until all the cheese is melted.
7. Let thicken and serve with sourdough bread.

Image found on page 46

Directions

1. In a stockpot or Dutch oven, place the following ingredients:
    - 2 cans condensed tomato soup
    - 2 cans water
    - 2 cups milk
    - ½ cup Parmesan cheese
    - 1 jar of canned tomatoes
2. Add the following spices:
    - 1 tsp. onion powder
    - ½ tsp. seasoned salt
    - ½ tsp. garlic powder
    - 1 tsp. basil
3. Whisk together.
4. Cook and drain ½ lb. of dried cheese-filled ravioli or tortellini. The dried pasta holds up better in the soup than frozen pasta.
5. Add pasta to pot and allow to simmer while making the grilled cheese.

Georges Briard

Chicken and Noodles

The perfect soup for when you are under the weather or any other time!

Ingredients

- cut of bone-in, skin-on chicken
- a couple of celery stalks with leaves attached
- 2–3 extra celery stalks for later
- a couple of unpeeled carrots
- 1 cut onion
- 8 cups water
- 3 chicken bouillon cubes
- 1 package of your favorite egg noodles (dried or frozen)
- seasoned salt
- extra chicken stock (if needed)

Directions

1. Add chicken (sprinkled with seasoned salt) vegetables, water, and bouillon cubes to a Crockpot and cook for 6 hours on low.
2. Strain liquid into a stockpot.
3. Discard the onion and celery. Keep the carrots, cut them up, and add back to the soup.
4. Remove and discard all the bones and skin from the chicken. Dice up the chicken and add to the soup.
5. In a separate stockpot, bring salted water to a boil. Dice the remaining stocks of celery and boil with the noodles until soft.
6. Drain the noodles and celery. Add to the soup.
7. Serve and enjoy!

Courtney's Chili

Everyone has their favorite chili recipe, and this one is mine. I like it a little sweet, and my husband likes it a little spicy. With this great base recipe, you can tailor it to your tastes.

Ingredients

- ½ lb. ground beef
- 3 sweet peppers, chopped
- ½ onion chopped
- 1 can pork and beans
- 1 can red kidney beans or chili beans
- 1 jar of canned tomatoes
- 1 tbs. steak seasoning
- 2 tbs. chili powder
- ½ tbs. seasoned salt
- 1 tsp. cumin
- 1 ½ tsp. onion powder
- 1 tsp. garlic powder
- ½ tsp. oregano

Directions

1. Brown ground beef. Remove and discard grease.
2. In a Dutch oven or stockpot, sauté peppers and onion until tender.
3. Add the beans, tomatoes, and ground beef.
4. Stir in the spices
5. Cover and let simmer for at least 10 minutes.
6. Serve with your favorite fixings! I like to add a little brown sugar, sour cream, grated cheddar cheese, and crushed crackers. My husband adds cayenne pepper, shredded cheese, and hot sauce.

Vegetable Couscous Soup

Goes oh so lovely with corn bread muffins!

Ingredients

- ¼ cup chopped onion
- 1–2 stalks celery diced
- 4–5 brussels sprouts, sliced, or ¼ cabbage, sliced
- 1 cup frozen green beans
- ½ cup frozen corn
- 1 cup frozen peas and carrots
- 1 cup tomato juice
- 1 can tomatoes
- 1 cup pearled couscous
- 1 package beefy onion dry soup mix
- 2 quarts beef stock or vegetable stock

Directions

1. In a stockpot or Dutch oven, sauté onion and celery until tender.
2. Add all the other vegetables to the pot.
3. Add the beef stock. You may also use vegetable stock if you're vegetarian.
4. Bring to a boil until all vegetables are tender.
5. Add the canned tomatoes and tomato juice.
6. Add 1 cup pearled couscous and allow to cook until doubled in size. If soup is too thick, add more beef stock and tomato juice.

When making cornbread muffins, add ½ cup sour cream and ½ cup shredded cheddar cheese to the mix before baking to add great flavor.

Sweet
Sweets

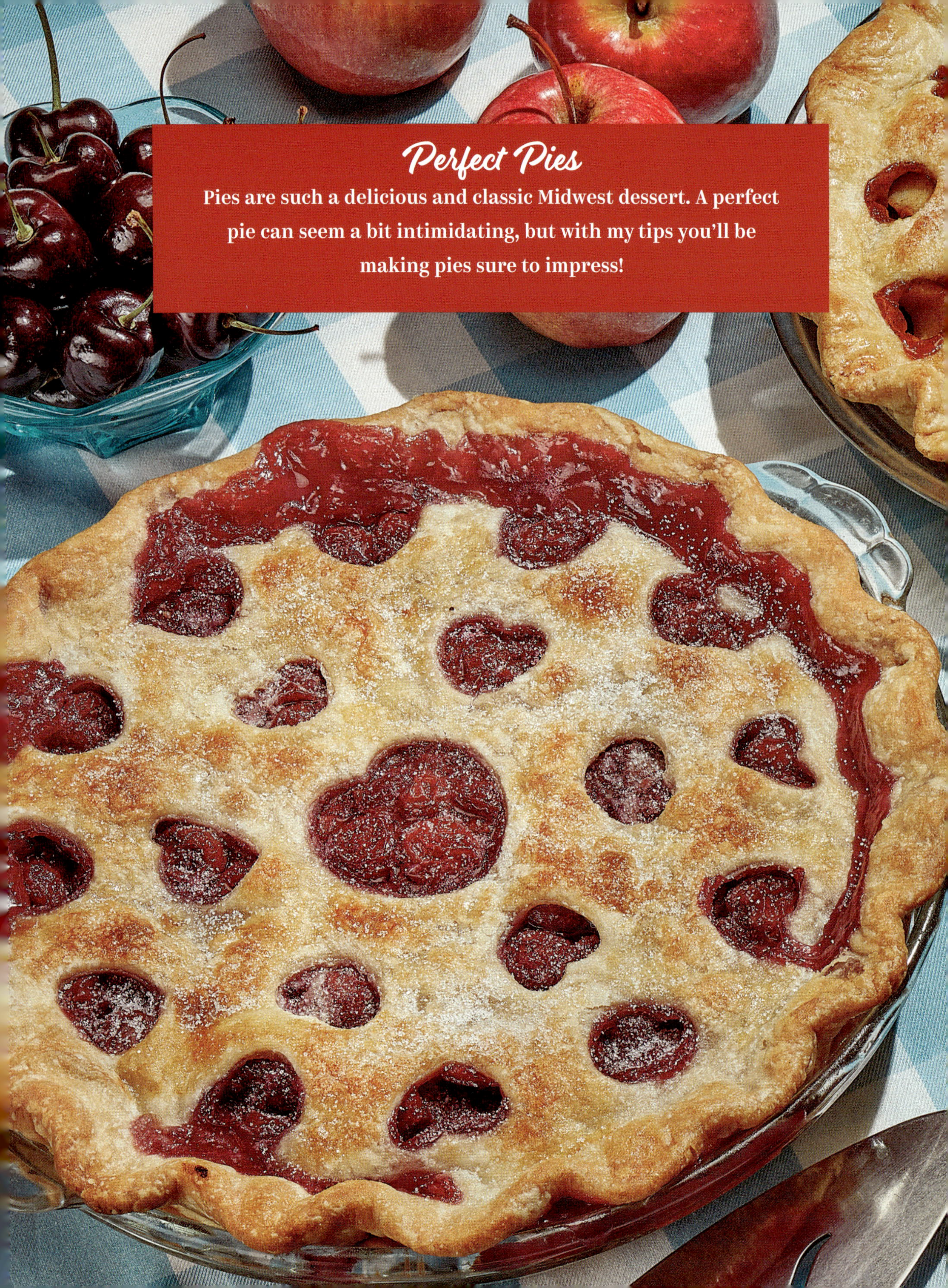

Perfect Pies

Pies are such a delicious and classic Midwest dessert. A perfect pie can seem a bit intimidating, but with my tips you'll be making pies sure to impress!

Piecrust

Ingredients

- 2 cups flour
- 1 tsp. salt
- ⅔ cup plus 2 tbs. shortening

Directions

1. Put all ingredients in a bowl and mix with fork.
2. Add cold water (5 tbs. or more). Mix until loosely combined.
3. Using your hands, form the dough into a ball.
4. Spank to combine. This allows the ingredients to mix without upsetting the delicate nature of the crust or disturbing the flakiness. Too much or too aggressive mixing can cause the crust to be tough.
5. Divide the crust into 2 balls.
6. Flatten and form into crust.
7. Yields 2 crusts.

Ingredients

- 2 piecrusts (one for top, one for bottom)
- 1 package thawed tart red cherries
- 1 cup sugar
- ⅓ cup flour
- ½ tsp. almond ext.
- 1 tbs. butter (for dotting)

Directions

1. Preheat oven to 400 degrees.
2. Combine sugar, cherries, flour, and almonds in a bowl.
3. Pour into bottom piecrust.
4. Dot with butter.
5. Add top crust.
6. Bake 35–45 minutes.

Peach Pie

Ingredients

- 2 piecrusts
- 1–2 packages thawed peach slices
- ⅔ cup sugar
- 2–3 tbs. flour
- ¼ tsp. cinnamon
- ¼ tsp. ground ginger

Directions

1. Preheat oven to 400 degrees.
2. Combine sugar, peaches, flour, and spices in a bowl.
3. Pour into bottom crust.
4. Dot with butter.
5. Add top crust.
6. Bake 40–50 minutes. When using fresh peaches, add a tbs. or 2 of flour.

Apple Pie

Ingredients

- 2 piecrusts
- 6 granny smith apples (peeled, cored, and thinly sliced)
- ¾ cup sugar
- 1 ½ tbs. flour
- 1 tsp. cinnamon
- ¾ tsp. nutmeg
- ¼ tsp. ground ginger

Directions

1. Preheat oven to 400.
2. Combine sugar, apples, flour, and spices in a bowl.
3. Pour into bottom crust.
4. Dot with butter.
5. Add top crust.
6. Bake 40–50 minutes.

Pie Tips

1. Cut a few slits in the top crust (in an aesthetically pleasing pattern) to allow air to escape while baking.
2. Trim the bottom crust flush with the edge of the pie pan.
3. On the top crust, leave about ½ inch of overhang all the way around. Fold the top edge under the bottom edge, folding them together, all the way around. Take both thumbs and press in while also pressing out with both index fingers (as shown in the pictures). Do this all the way around to form a perfect flute, which is sure to impress!
4. Brush the top crust with milk and sprinkle with sugar before baking. This gives your crust a nice sheen and a light crisp.
5. Bake with a crust cover (make one out of foil if you don't have one) for the first 35 minutes, then remove for the last 10–15 minutes. This keeps the crust from getting burnt.

Cinnamon Sugar Piecrust

My mom and Grandma Smith always made this for us as kids when we were waiting for the pie to ready. Now I have passed on the tradition to my kids, and they look forward to this little treat each time I bake a pie.

Directions

1. Combine crust scraps and roll out on a baking sheet.
2. Spread with butter and sprinkle with cinnamon and sugar.
3. Bake at same temperature as whatever pie you are making for 10–15 minutes.
4. Cut into pieces and enjoy as a snack while you wait for the pie to bake!

Retro
HAPPY BIRTHDAY
Retro

World's Best Sugar Cookies

Seriously, these are the best sugar cookies ever! I use Mexican vanilla in all my baking. I just love the flavor, but you can add regular vanilla as well.

Ingredients

- ½ cup powdered sugar
- ½ cup white sugar
- ½ cup butter
- ½ cup oil
- 1 egg
- ½ tsp. almond extract
- 1 tsp. vanilla
- ½ tsp. salt
- ½ tsp. baking soda
- ½ tsp. cream of tartar
- 2 ½ cup flour

Directions

1. Cream sugars, butter, and oil until light and fluffy.
2. Add egg, vanilla, and almond. Beat until combined.
3. Add baking soda, cream of tartar, and salt. Mix thoroughly.
4. Lastly, add the flour and mix until dough forms into a ball and pulls away from sides of bowl. Start with 2 cups flour—weather and humidity can affect the flour density. You may need to go up to 3 cups. Just make sure the dough forms a ball and pulls away from the sides.
5. Turn out onto a plate. Cover and place in refrigerator for 1 hour to chill.
6. Roll out dough on a floured surface and cut into desired shapes. I usually put flour on top of the dough and on the rolling pin to help prevent sticking.
7. Bake at 350 degrees for 8–10 minutes.
8. Let cool and frost.
9. Store in an airtight container for up to 1 week. Yields about 2 dozen cookies.

Basic Buttercream Frosting

Cut recipe in half for sugar cookies; make full recipe for cupcakes; double ingredients for a cake that you frost down the sides and in between layers.

Ingredients

- 1 stick softened butter
- 4 cups powdered sugar
- up to ¼ cup water
- 1 tsp. vanilla extract, clear
- food coloring

Directions

1. Mix butter, vanilla, and powdered sugar in mixer with whisk attachment.
2. Add small amounts of water until you reach desired consistency.
3. Add color and mix until dispersed.

Ingredients

- 2 ½ tbs. water
- 2 cup powdered sugar
- 1 tbs. Wilton Meringue Powder
- ¼– ½ tsp. clear vanilla extract
- ¼– ½ tsp. butter extract

Directions

1. Mix in stand mixer on low for 5 minutes until smooth. Add more or less water to get the consistency you desire (thicker for outlines; thinner for easier low).
2. Divide, color, and decorate. I like to use squeeze bottles for this! Allow to harden for several hours before touching.
3. Store in airtight containers.
4. Add more water as you decorate if icing starts to get too thick.

S'mores Cookie Bars

Ingredients

- 1 stick butter, softened
- ¾ cup sugar
- 1 egg
- 1 tsp. vanilla
- 1 ⅓ cup flour
- ¾ cup graham crackers, crushed
- 1 tsp. baking powder
- ¼ tsp. salt
- 4 milk chocolate candy bars
- 1 cup mini marshmallows

Directions

1. Preheat oven to 350 degrees.
2. Grease an 8x8 glass baking dish.
3. Beat butter and sugar in a large bowl until light and fluffy.
4. Add egg and vanilla. Beat well.
5. Add baking powder and salt. Mix well.
6. Add flour and graham crackers. Mix again.
7. Press half of the dough into the dish.
8. Arrange chocolate bars over the dough, breaking apart as needed to fit.
9. Sprinkle marshmallows over the top.
10. Scatter bits of remaining dough over marshmallows and carefully press to form a layer.
11. Bake 30–45 minutes or until lightly brown.
12. Let cool and cut into bars.

Banana Split Dessert

A classic Midwest potluck dessert recipe, and with good reason—it's delicious!

Ingredients

Crust

- 2 cups crushed vanilla wafers
- 1 stick melted butter
- ½ cup powdered sugar

1. Combine and shape into an oblong glass baking dish.

Filling

- 8 oz. softened cream cheese
- 2 cups powdered sugar
- 1 stick softened butter
- ½ tsp. vanilla extract

Directions

1. Mix together until smooth and pour over crust.
   Top with the following layers:

- crushed pineapple
- 3 bananas, sliced
- whipped cream
- chopped peanuts
- chocolate syrup drizzle
- chopped maraschino cherries

Cravory Cocktails

Mai Tai

Ingredients

- 2 oz. dark rum
- 1 oz. triple sec
- 1 oz. orange juice
- 2 ½ oz. pineapple juice
- ½ oz. grenadine

Directions

1. Fill glass with ice.
2. Pour in rum and triple sec.
3. Slowly pour juices on top of the rum, pouring down the side of the glass or down a stirring stick. This helps to keep the classic separated look of a mai tai.
4. Add grenadine and garnish with pineapple or tiny paper umbrella.
5. Enjoy!

Ingredients

- 1.5 liter moscato
- 1 cup peach schnapps
- ½ cup rum
- 2 cups pineapple-orange juice
- 6 oz. pineapple juice
- 2 oranges, sliced
- 1 apple, sliced
- 1 lemon, sliced
- 1 lime, sliced
- 4–5 strawberries, sliced

Directions

1. Mix all ingredients together and refrigerate overnight.
2. Serve each glass with a little soda water or Sprite to add some fizz.

Bloody Mary

Ingredients

- 6 oz. tomato juice
- 2 oz. tomato vodka
- 1 oz. lemon juice
- 1 ½ oz. Worcestershire sauce
- 1 ½ oz. dill pickle juice
- Salt and pepper to taste

Directions

1. In a tall mixing glass, add all ingredients and stir.
2. Pour over a glass of ice.
3. Serve with optional vegetable garnishes.

To make tomato vodka, place chopped tomatoes in a jar. Fill jar with vodka and allow to sit for 1–2 weeks. Drain and store the infused tomato vodka.

Hot Toddy

Ingredients

- 1 oz. honey
- 1 ½ oz. bourbon
- lemon

Directions

1. In a glass, place honey and bourbon.
2. Cut lemon in half and squeeze into drink to taste.
3. Warm in microwave for 30 seconds.
4. Stir to combine.

Perfect cocktail to warm you up or help you get over a cold.

Ryan's Margars (Margaritas)

Ingredients

- 2 oz. añejo tequila
- 1 ½ oz. simple syrup
- 1 ½ oz. orange liqueur
- 1 oz. of fresh citrus juice (lemon, orange, and lime)

Directions

Recommended to triple recipe for 2 people.

1. Put all ingredients in a cocktail shaker filled with ice. Shake vigorously.
2. Pour over ice in salted-rim glass.
3. Serve with citrus garnish.

Sazerac

Ingredients

- absinthe for glass rinse
- 1 sugar cube or spoonful of sugar, muddled
- 2–3 dashes of Peychaud's bitters
- 2 ½ oz. rye whiskey
- lemon rind

Directions

1. Do an absinthe rinse on the glass (coat the inside of the glass with absinthe).
2. In a separate tall mixing glass, add sugar, bitters, and ½ oz. of whiskey. Muddle and mix to dissolve the sugar.
3. Fill the mixing glass with ice. Add the other 2 oz. whiskey and thoroughly stir with a cocktail spoon and set aside.
4. Shave off a piece of lemon rind. Rim the drinking glass.
5. Strain cocktail into drinking glass.
6. Garnish with lemon rind.

Old-Fashioned

Ingredients

- orange
- bourbon
- cocktail cherries
- spoonful of sugar
- Angostura bitters

Directions

1. Place sugar in the bottom of drinking glass.
2. Add ½ oz. hot water. Stir to dissolve sugar.
3. Add a couple of dashes of bitters to glass.

4. Cut an orange wheel. Place in the bottom of the drinking glass.
5. Add 2 flavored cherries. Muddle fruit and sugar.
6. Fill glass with ice.
7. Pour in 2 ½ oz. bourbon. Stir thoroughly.
8. Garnish with orange wheel and cherry.

Optional: add fresh-squeezed orange juice and/or flavored cherry juice before adding bourbon.

Glossary

1. **Cream:** Mixing butter and sugar(s) together until well blended, leaving you with a fluffy, light yellow mix.

2. **Sift:** The preparation procedure of passing a dry ingredient, such as flour or sugar, through a mesh-bottom sieve. This process combines air with the ingredient.

3. **Roux:** A flour and fat cooked together and used to thicken sauces.

4. **Deglaze:** A cooking technique for removing and dissolving browned food residue from a pan to flavor sauces, soups, and gravies.

5. **Reduce or Reduction:** The process of thickening and intensifying the flavor of a liquid mixture, such as a soup, sauce, wine, or juice, by simmering or boiling.

6. **Caramelized onions:** Sautéing onion slices in oil until dark brown but not burnt. It brings out the sweetness of the onion.

7. **Baste:** A cooking technique that involves cooking meat with either its own juices or some type of preparation, such as a sauce or marinade.

8. **Dredge:** A cooking technique used to coat wet or moist foods with a dry ingredient, such as flour, prior to cooking.

9. **Butterfly cut:** A term used to describe a piece of fish or cut of meat that has been cut open with the sides spread apart, resembling butterfly wings.

About the Author

My name is Courtney Hill.

I grew up in a smaller town in the Midwest, then moved to the city in my adult years. I learned most of what I know about cooking from my mother, who learned from her mother. I didn't grow up on the farm, but I have relatives who are farmers and, well, let's just say we know a thing or two about good food! I learned the rest of my cooking knowledge from my formal education.

I have a master's degree in family and consumer sciences (FCS), and I taught high school FCS for four years. I decided to stay home when my twins were born, and I loved being home with them. I still love teaching and the FCS umbrella of subjects. I think they are essential and teach us how to become functioning adults and members of society. I approach my recipes with an educator's mindset. Hopefully you find them easy to follow and easy to prepare.

I am married to my love. We have been married since 2005. He is a very talented commercial photographer. I work at the photography studio as the studio manager and chief financial officer. We have two children—fraternal twins. Being twins has its unique joys and challenges, and we love them very much!

I am a very crafty person, and I love to create and work with my hands. My hobbies include knitting, crocheting, cross-stitch and embroidery, sewing, quilting, canning, gardening, cooking, baking, and cookie and cake decorating. I also love to throw pottery but haven't found the time in the last few years. I am a mid-century girl at heart. I love the fifties and anything vintage. Some of my favorite pastimes are thrifting and antiquing. The theme of my cookbook definitely has the midcentury vintage vibe that I love, and so do a lot of my recipes!

While I was a stay-at-home mom, I found myself slipping away a bit. I was knee-deep in dirty diapers and schedules. I needed to do something for myself as a creative outlet. So I created a video cooking blog to share my recipes and teach people how to cook simple and delicious meals for their families. I started it in January 2015 and have enjoyed every minute of it. This cookbook is a companion to the blog. I hope you enjoy the recipes and check out the how-to videos on my blog: www.cookhomemade.net.

I want to inspire and teach a new generation how to cook great meals at home for themselves and their families. I want to bring back family meals and time spent together with Mom or Dad in the kitchen preparing them. I bring a modern spin to classic vintage-style recipes.

I love being from the Midwest. It's the heart of the country, and there is so much wide-open space, even in the city. A lot of my recipes are inspired by my Midwest roots. I hope this cookbook gives you some staple recipes you will share with your families. Enjoy the food and the time together!

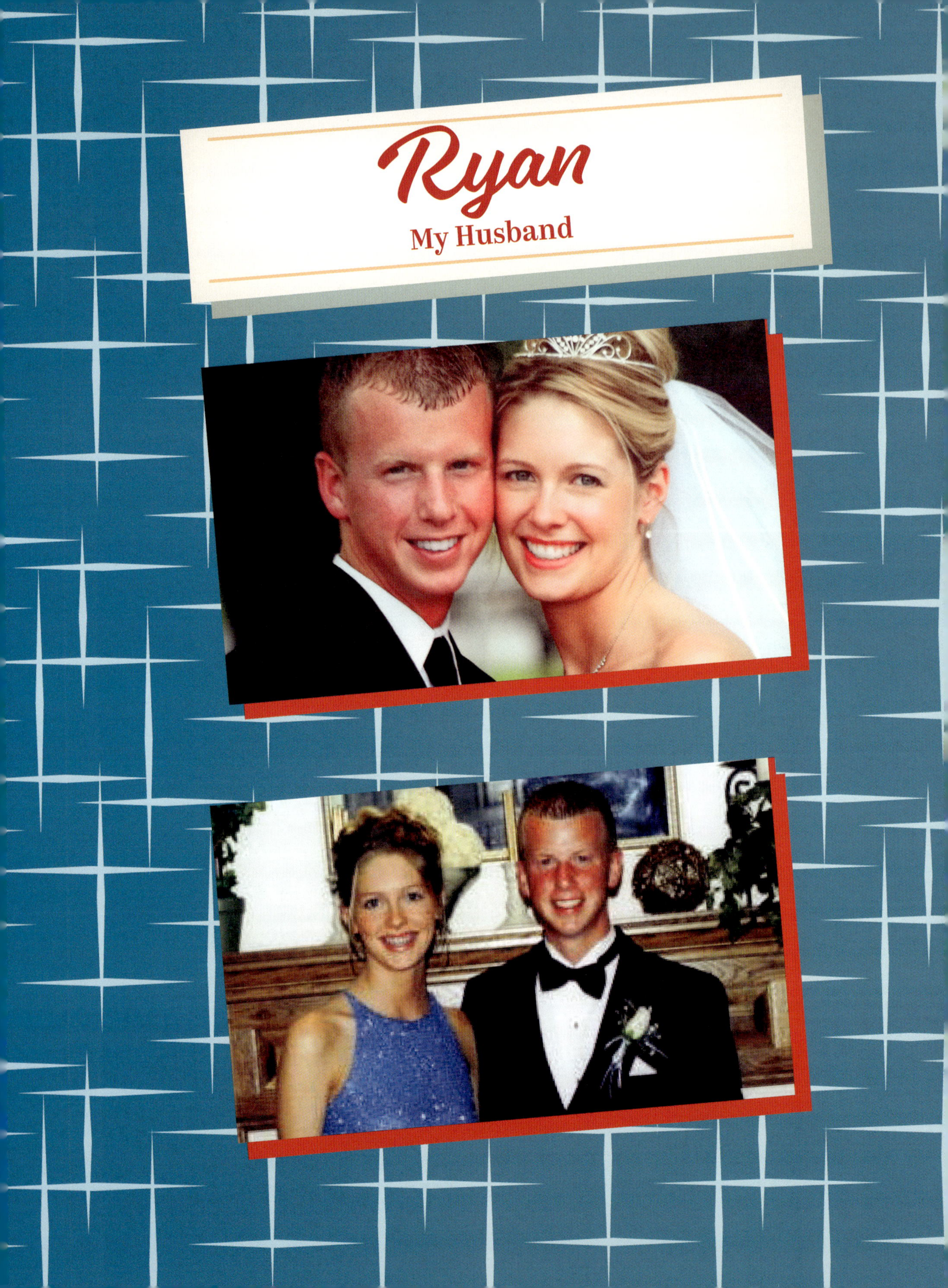
Ryan
My Husband

Carrie
My Mom

Grandma Lois
My Mom's Mom

GG Barbara
My Dad's Mom

Abbreviations

1 lb .... pound

C .... degrees Celsius

Qt .... quart

c .... cup

in. .... inch

F .... degrees Fahrenheit

Tsp or t .... teaspoon

L .... liter

gal .... gallon

Tbsp or t .... tablespoon

Fl. oz .... fluid ounce

Pt .... pint

Doz .... dozen (equals 12)

Common Substitutions

Ingredient	Substitution
1 tsp all spice	½ t cinnamon + ½ tsp ground cloves
1 tsp baking powder	½ tsp baking soda + ½ tsp cream of tartar
1 Tbsp butter	1 T oil, or 1 T shortening
1 cup buttermilk	1 cup milk + 1 Tbsp vinegar
1 cup heavy cream (not for whipping cream)	¾ cup milk + ⅓ cup butter
1 tsp dried herbs	1 tsp fresh herbs
1 cup self rising flour	1 cup flour + 1½ tsp baking powder ½ tsp salt
1 Tbsp lemon juice	½ Tbsp vinegar
1 cup brown sugar	1 cup sugar or ⅞ cup sugar + 1 Tbsp molasses

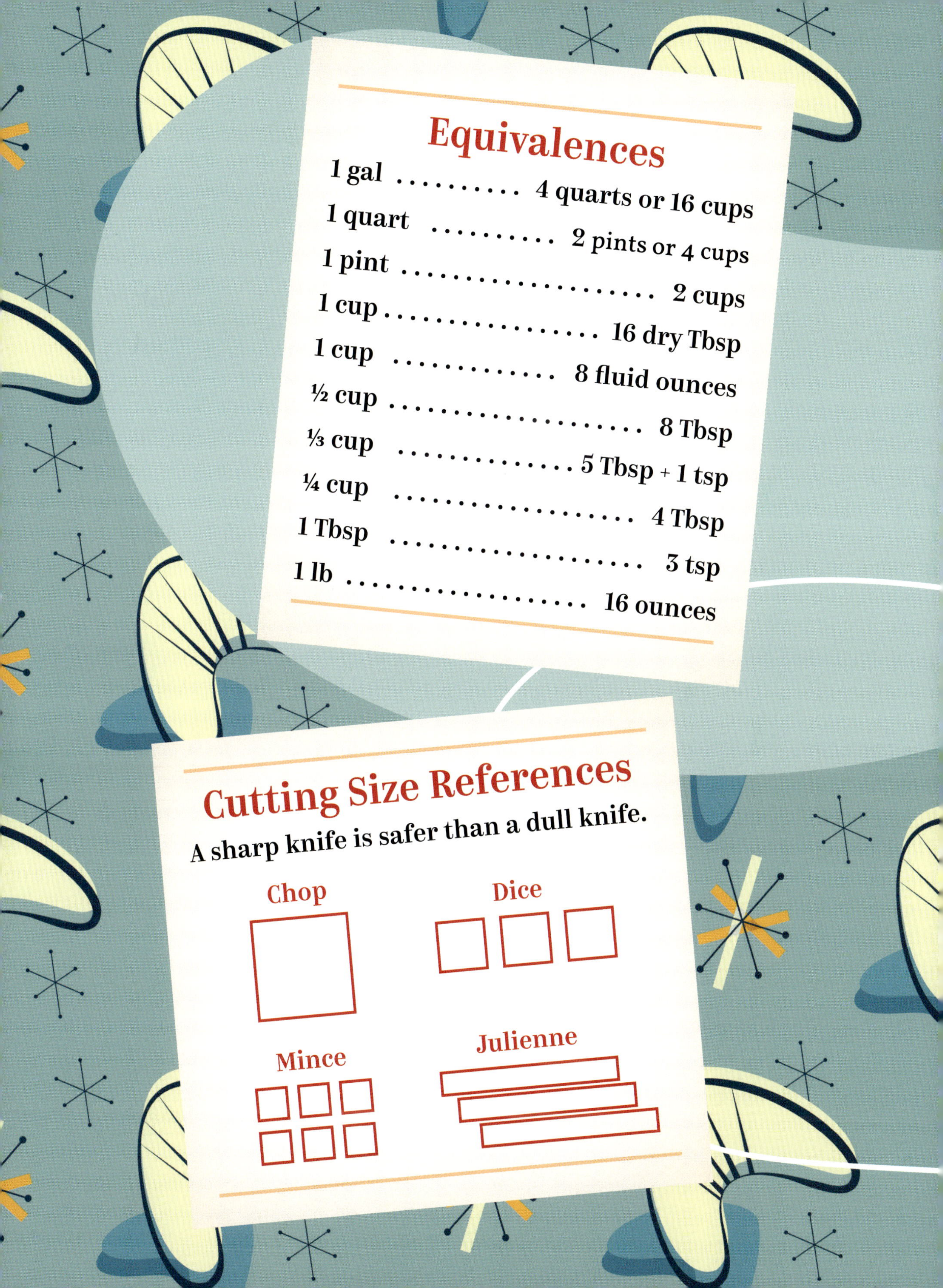

Equivalences

1 gal	4 quarts or 16 cups
1 quart	2 pints or 4 cups
1 pint	2 cups
1 cup	16 dry Tbsp
1 cup	8 fluid ounces
½ cup	8 Tbsp
⅓ cup	5 Tbsp + 1 tsp
¼ cup	4 Tbsp
1 Tbsp	3 tsp
1 lb	16 ounces

Cutting Size References

A sharp knife is safer than a dull knife.